Maria L Stewart

Our Little Brown House

A Poem

Maria L Stewart

Our Little Brown House
A Poem

ISBN/EAN: 9783744710435

Printed in Europe, USA, Canada, Australia, Japan

Cover: Foto ©Thomas Meinert / pixelio.de

More available books at **www.hansebooks.com**

OUR LITTLE BROWN HOUSE;

A Poem of West Point.

WRITTEN FOR THE NEW YEAR'S FESTIVAL AT THE CADETS' SABBATH-SCHOOL
OF THE METHODIST EPISCOPAL CHURCH,

JANUARY 1, 1879,

AND READ ON THAT OCCASION BY
THE AUTHORESS, (M. L. S.)

NEW YORK:
PUBLISHED BY F. KALKHOFF, Jr.
1880.

PREFACE.

These poems were prepared merely with the hope of interesting the members of the Sabbath-School before whom they were read, and were not intended for publication. At the urgent request of many friends, however, I have been induced to present them to the public in their present form.

M. L. S.

OUR LITTLE BROWN HOUSE.
(Drawn by William Erwin.)

OUR LITTLE BROWN HOUSE.

THERE'S a little brown house just under the hill ;
It's not by the river, nor yet by a rill ;
Its not on the green-sward where the gay and proud meet,
But it stands on the corner of Bandbarrack's street.

This time-honored veteran, in armor complete,
Has stood many winters the storm and the sleet—
The early spring rains and the long summer heat,
The wear and the tear of a great many feet.

It's a very small building, and plain in its way ;
No high-toned paintings, not a thing that is gay ;
It was built of the gun-house of Col Thayer fame,
During the years of the Delafield reign.

Our Little Brown House.

Then came Captain B.—he thought it all wrong
That such a small house should hold such a throng ;
So out went the walls, up went the roof,
And thus it was altered and made large enough.

Then again it was altered, with the door to the south,
Which did very well in time of a drought ;
Then Lieutenant G., he thought it to better—
He changed it a little, but not to the letter.

It was painted without and papered within ;
The roof now is shingles, then it was tin.
Next came Colonel B., a thrifty man—
He too had to lend a helping hand.

So down went the stove and up went a heater,
A thing which, indeed, was very much neater.
Again it's been altered, just right, it's confess't,
For the door has gone back again into the west.

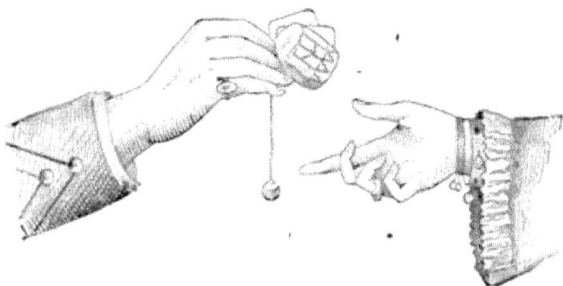

PRESENTING "SPOONEY BUTTON."
(Sketched by Cadet Cameron, Class of '83.)

Our Little Brown House.

The east end's been paneled, and looks very good ;
The door has been covered with a very nice hood ;
And thus it's been altered again and again ;
This time it was altered to keep off the rain.

This little brown house, so dear to each heart,
So famous in history, so free from all art—
Our hearts with emotion always will thrill
When we think of the chapel under the hill.

But where are the loved ones we met here of yore?
Their forms and their faces we'll see nevermore ;
Their loud, cheery laugh and swift-coming feet
No more in the Sabbath-school ever to greet.

Some have launched out on the world's busy tide,
Some have got married, some have died,
Some on the frontier, wading through strife,
With the musketry's rattle and the wild scalper's knife.

Our Little Brown House.

Some by the camp-fires, with their minds on the rack,
Eating salt pork with a little hard-tack,
Wading through snow or fording a river,
Or asleep on the ground without any cover.

From the falls of Missouri, with its loud, maddening roar,
To the slopes of Pacific, an ever-green shore,
To the Atlantic Ocean, with a coast sand-bound,
There some of my boys are sure to be found.

To the northward, to the westward, and fair, sunny south,
Like the dove with the olive-branch of peace in its mouth,
Thus they've gone forth their garlands to weave,
When they get through they'll return with the sheaves.

Some on the Lone Star, quite at their ease,
Eating their rations, doing just as they please,
Basking in sunshine among the sweet flowers,
Whiling away the long, tedious hours.

KOSCIUSZKO GARDEN.

Our Little Brown House.

From the St. Lawrence River to the Rio Grande,
From Puget's Sound to Maine's cold sand,
O'er the hilltops, through the valleys, never to lag,
Not a spot on this land but they've planted the flag.

————•————

The old village people—where are they,
That in the chapel met to pray?
The stalwart man and maiden mild,
The matron and the little child,

The son and sire side by side,
As to the village church they hied—
Some are gone and sweetly rest,
With their white hands folded on their breast.

Under the violet and the rose,
The autumn leaves and winter snows,
On the banks of the Hudson there to sleep,
While the moon and stars their vigils keep.

Our Little Brown House.

The man of God, with modest mien,
With faltering steps and looks serene,
As to the sacred desk they knelt
And poured forth what their spirits felt,

Their hearts went up with pure desire,
While on the altar burned the fire ;
A few still linger on the shore,
Veterans of a holy war.

May this little brown house, of good constitution,
Built on the classic grounds of the old Revolution,
The Stars and the Stripes, the blue and cadet grey,
Be the last things to perish when time's passed away.

SUPPLEMENT.

To the young gentlemen that are here with us now—
To you and the rest I make my best bow.
Now listen, young men ; take heed what I say ;
Your time is coming, it's not far away.

Be true to your trust and your old Alma Mater ;
Lean firm on that arm, you'll need nothing better :
And to the young gentlemen of the Tenth Section,
Flee to the Fourth—in it there's protection.

Perhaps that will do, but the Ninth, I am told,
Will send the young gentlemen out in the cold.
There are three honest men of old cadet fame—
Phil, Math and Chem, I think is their name.

FLIRTATION PATH.

(Photographed by G. W. Pack.)

Our Little Brown House.

These three honest fellows are all very bold,
And are sure to kick somebody out of the fold ;
Then off goes the trimmings, and away goes the grey,
And then you are told to get out of the way.

Then you'll think of Flirtation and old Gee's rock,
And the place where you sat with your Sweet Four O'clock ;
Then you'll think of the taffy made over the gas,
Of the butter and sugar you hived from the mess.

Now when to the blackboard for trial you stand,
Keep steady, be ready, your chalk in your hand.
Don't think of failing ; stand well on your ground ;
Don't let it be said—a man has been found.

———————•———————

This poem is respectfully dedicated to the Corps of Cadets, by

THEIR MATERNAL FRIEND.

THE BARRACKS.
(Photographed by G. W. Pack.)

GRAND CELEBRATION.

With Pyrotechnic Lights, at the Military Academy, by Santa Claus,
12 o'clock, 1880.

HARK ! what's that that bursts on the midnight air ?
" The Cadets are loose," said a lady fair.
"Cadets loose ?" echoed her puzzled spouse,
 As he rose in haste and donned his clothes.

From " Siege Gun Battery" came a roar
That echoed back from shore to shore,
Rumbling along under old Cro' Nest,
And sunk in the far-off hills to rest.

Just at this juncture came pouring forth
From every window in the north
Of the Barrack building grim and gray,
And chased the moonbeams out of the way,

Grand Celebration.

The grandest sight that ever was seen,
Or ever will be again, I ween,—
Rockets, Roman Candles and Blue Lights clear,
To welcome in the glad New Year.

With the booming of cannon and grand "fish-horn"
Eighteen hundred and eighty was born ;
This fine little fellow was ushered in
With rocket's roar and fish-horn's din.

What means this noise and running around,
Looking for something that's not to be found ?
For every door was relieved of its handle
By some friend, of course, surely not by a vandal,

To keep intruders who were stalking around
From wakening the boys who were sleeping so sound,
Dreaming of fish-horns and other such things
That Santa Claus always to the children brings.

THE COLOR GUARD.

(By Cadet Cameron, Class of '83.)

Grand Celebration.

Just at this moment came a loud crash—
A window is broken in with a smash,
And a voice calls out, " Bring me an axe!"
And on his near neighbor he levied the tax.

I'll let him see, thought the neighbor, who'll lift the latch,
As he handed him out the innocent match;
The reason was this, St. Nick had been busy an hour or more,
And that was the reason he'd fastened the door.

'Tis the midnight hour; the Long Roll has beat,
And brought every boy in a jiff to his feet,
In the area of the Barracks, on the cold, damp ground,
And not a delinquent is to be found,

Except the little fellow who was locked in his room
By some naughty boy, and of course could not come.
From the hall-ways came running, all loose to be sure,
Every boy, in a hurry his place to secure,

Grand Celebration.

And there on the cold ground, in the night air to stand,
While the searchers were looking for things contraband.
In a room two Rockets were picked up by a scout,
That Santa Claus dropped as he made his way out,

While up in the cockloft, so cosy and snug,
Lay the old brass cannon, like a " bug in a rug,"
Where Santa Claus left it to be raised up higher,
And then, after all, the old thing hung fire.

What can be the matter? what's all this about ?
That every boy from his bed is turned out
In the night air to shiver and freeze,
With nought on his feet but his old Reveilles ?

There to wait for a long half hour
Still as the bell in the old clock tower ;
The scouts and the searchers have all done their best,
And the boys are allowed to return to their rest,

MAKING TAFFY AFTER TAPS.

(Sketched by Cadet Hall, Class of '83.)

Grand Celebration.

And all tumble into their little cot beds,
While visions of "Calling Day" float through their heads,
Sleeping and snoring like other good boys,
For Santa Claus had filled all their stockings with toys.

But lo! from the roof comes a thundering noise,
Loud enough to waken all of the boys;
That old brass cannon had crept out of its lair,
In the Grand Celebration determined to share.

From the roof of the Barracks dark and gray
The old brass cannon blazed away,
Waking the neighbors far and near,
To let them know there was nothing to fear;

For old St. Nick had done his work,
And into his sleigh had skipped with a jerk;
And calling by name each tiny reindeer,
As he rode out of sight he cried "Happy New Year."

Dedicated to all the "Boys" who took part in the "Grand Celebration," by

SANTA CLAUS.

www.ingramcontent.com/pod-product-compliance
Lightning Source LLC
Chambersburg PA
CBHW021549270326
41930CB00008B/1431